Wine Labels

Vintage Pictures and advertising

Retro Books

Presentation

This book consists of a non-systematic series of images to collect, see, and, above all, to use for decoration purposes.

It was designed so that you can detach all images or each one individually, allowing you to frame the pictures you like the most.

The purpose of this book is aesthetic only, to assemble together beautiful images which take us to charming places in the history of great brands of food and drinking products. It is a tribute to so many advertisement creators and label designers that will forever remain in our memories.

For this reason, we do not indicate dates or researches that we made throughout the process of making this book.

Retro Books

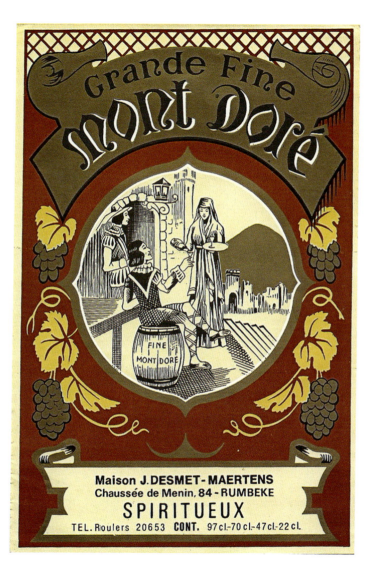

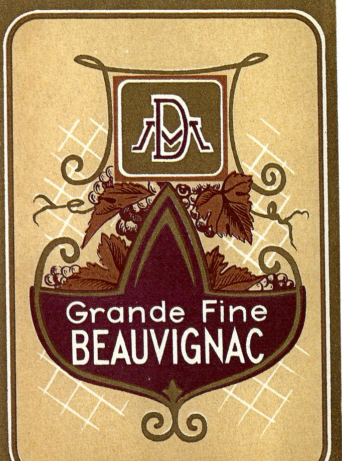

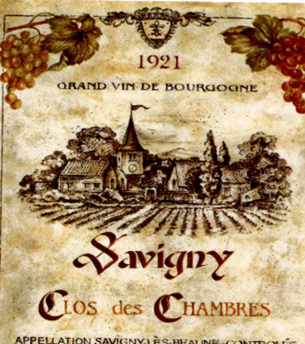

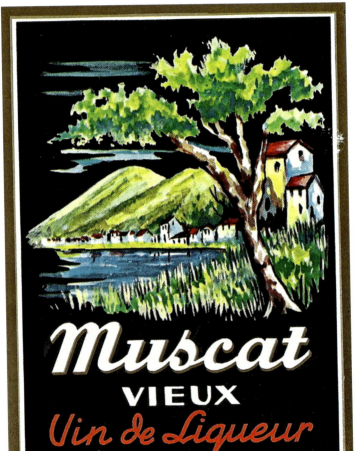

Domaine de Laroche

SPIRITUEUX

Fine
SUPÉRIEURE

Cont. 98 cl. 48   R. C. Courtrai 78.466

Wij waarborgen de natuurlijke sterkte van de geestrijke drank die geen enkel kunstmatig versterkingsmiddel bevat. Door zijn oorsprong schaadt hij de gezondheid niet, veroorzaakt geen maag- of andere pijnen, is zeer verteerbaar en is een afdoend geneesmiddel tegen vele ziekten.

Anc. Ets. Rob. Dewaegenare 8600 Menin   Maison fondée 1899

VIN BLANC
VANDA

Sucré

des Caves Vanda

Firma **VAN DER ZANDE** *Nieuwpoort*

INHOUD ∓ 72 CL.   WAARB. 4 FR.   H. R. V. 13820

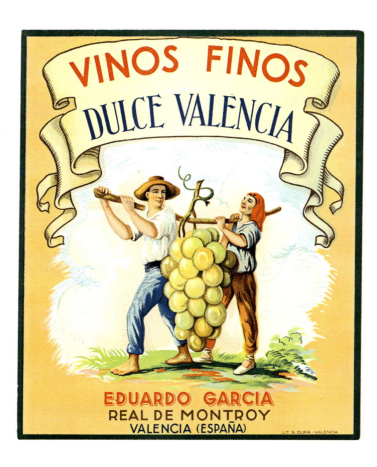

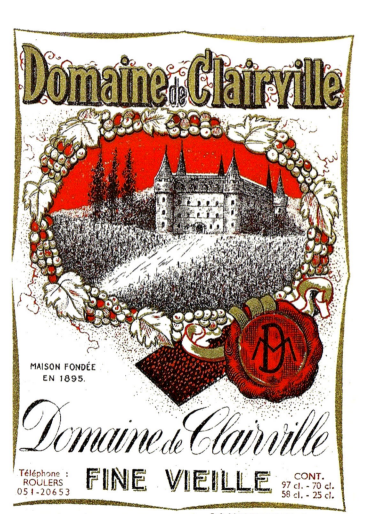

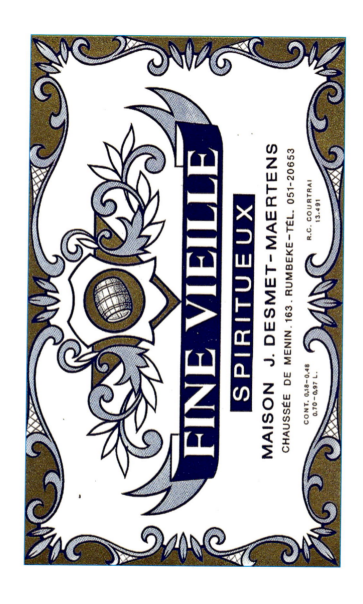

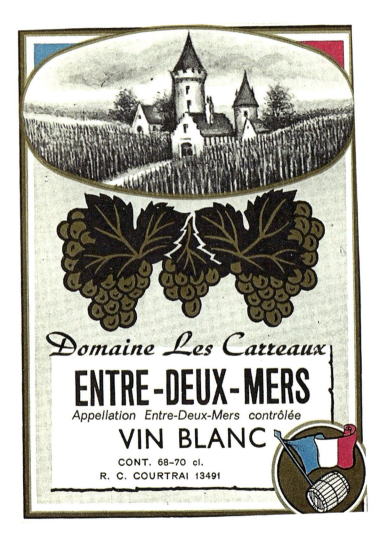

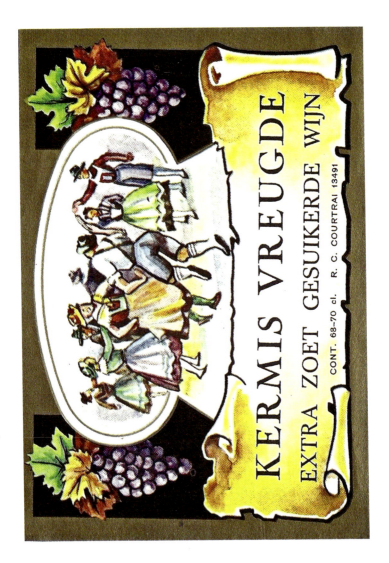

Vieille Fine

LES CAVES RÉUNIES

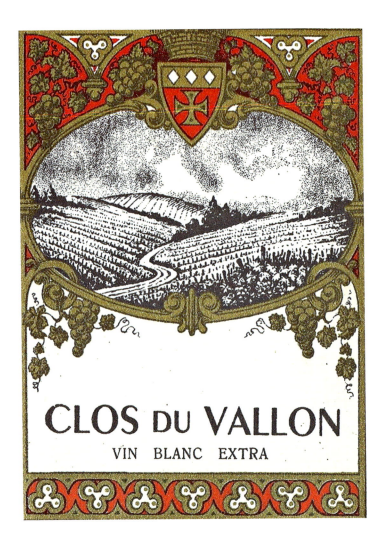

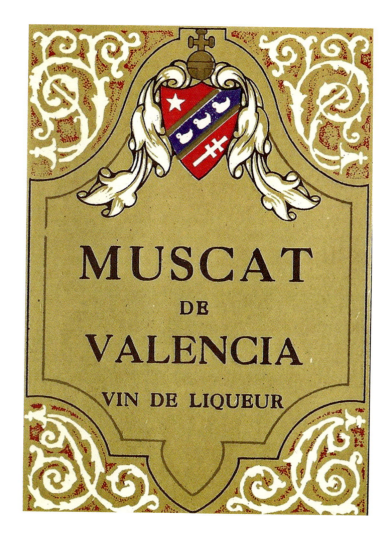

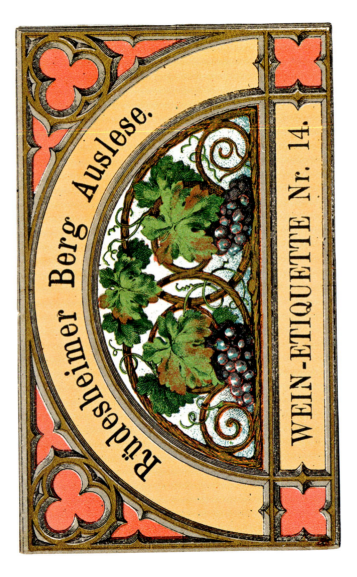

SPECIAL

★★★★★

SELECTION

WHITE SWAN

PRODUCE OF FRANCE

PURE FRENCH BRANDY

MAISON FONDÉE
EN 1826

SPECIAL SELECTION

SELECTED AND BOTTLED BY **CHEMINEAUD FRÈRES** BORDEAUX FRANCE

43° G.L.   0,35 L.

EMB 16102 F

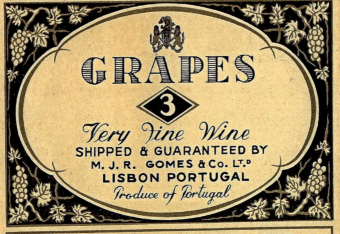

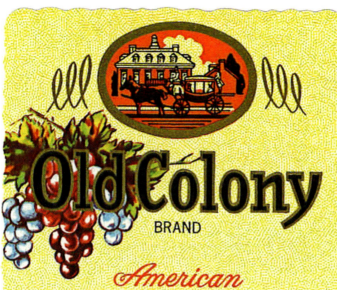

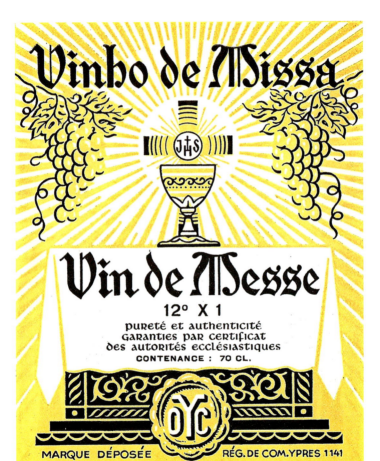

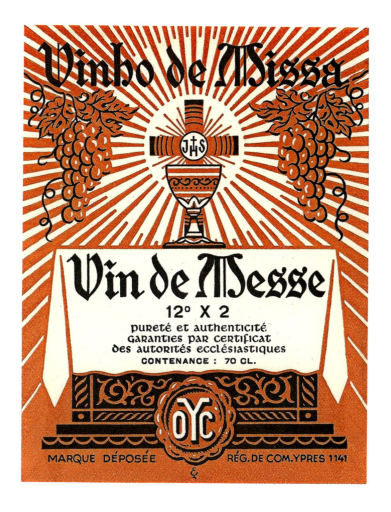

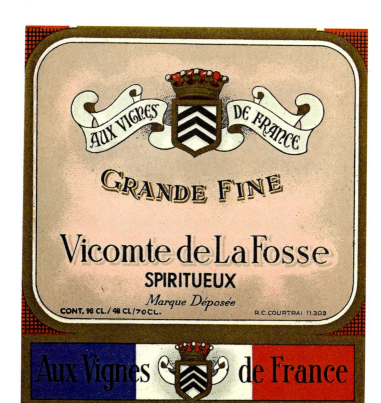

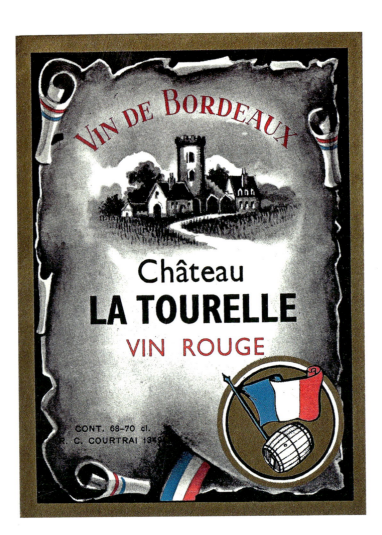

VIN ROUGE

SUPERIEUR

CONT.: 70 CL.

H.R. GENT 19885

Domaine St Louis

GRAND VIN
BLANC - DEMI-DOUX

R. C. Y. 1141

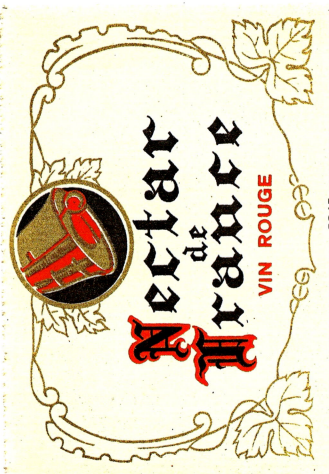

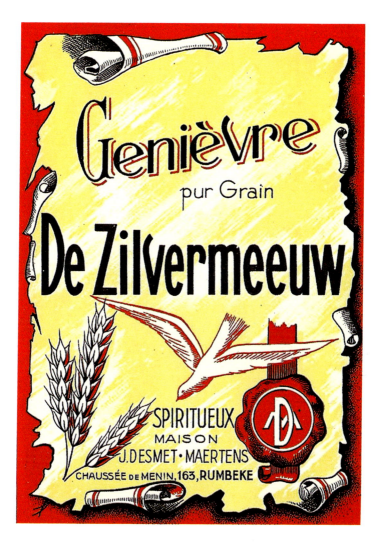

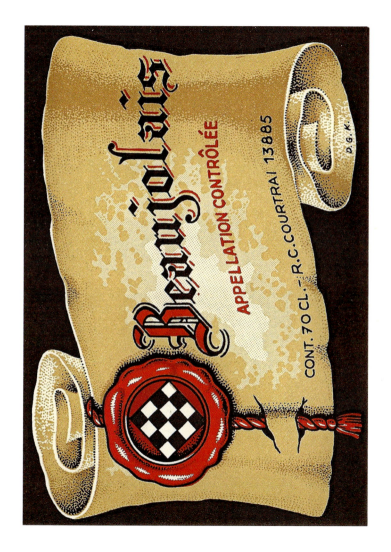

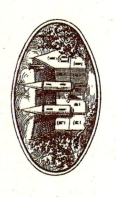

GRAND VIN ROUGE
SELECTIONNÉ

CONT. 0,70 L.

H. R. 5245

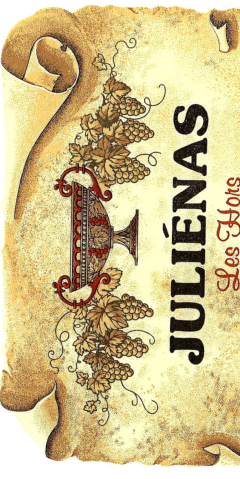

MANOIR DE GOURNAC
VIN ROUGE
MONOPOLE

CONT. 70 cl.

R.C. Courtrai 11303

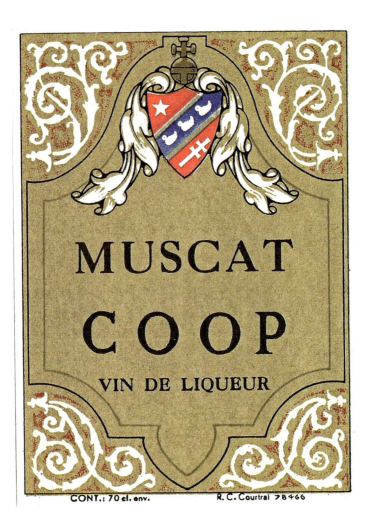

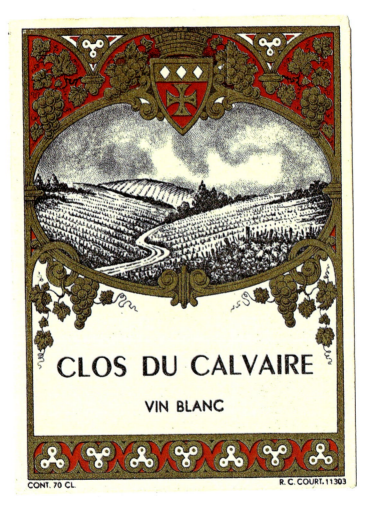

VINHO DE MESA

CLARETE

M. J. R. GOMES & C.ª

VALADARES   PORTUGAL

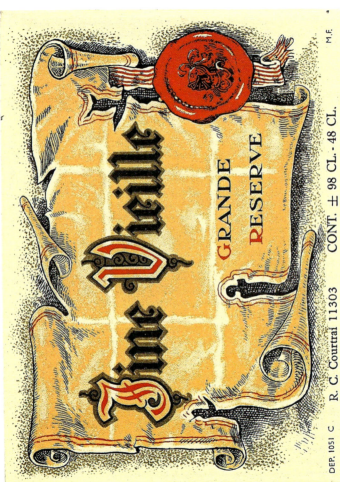

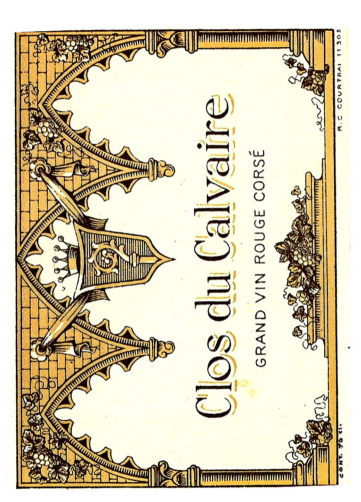

VIN ROUGE

H.R.K. 13491   INH. 3/4 L. 1/1 L.

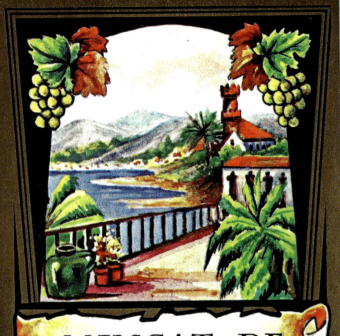

35° ENV.

CHRIJSMER & C?

FINE EXTRA

SPIRITUEUX INDIGÈNE

FRS. LE LITRE·   FRS ¾ LITRE·   FRS ½ LITRE.

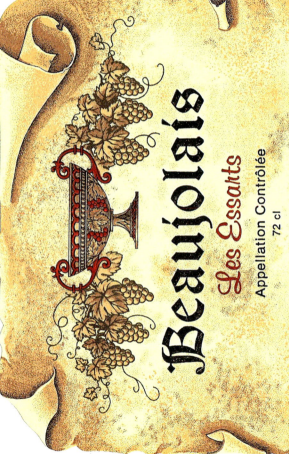

Cloche de France

VIN BLANC SUCRÉ

CONT: 70 CL.   REG. DE COMM. 5245 KORTRIJK.

Retro Books

Unit 16 & 17. 12F, Tower A
New Mandarim Plaza,14
Science Museum Rd. TST East
Kowloon, Hong Kong

Printed in Chine